BEST-EVER
CHRISTMAS
NEW GIFTS & IDEAS

KÖNEMANN

Christmas Menus

Cold Buffet for 12

Shrimp with Fresh Herb Dip
Mushroom and Thyme Pate
Glazed Leg of Ham
Chicken and Apricot Terrine
Vegetable Slaw with Mustard Mayonnaise
Leafy Green Salad with Walnut Dressing
Wild and Brown Rice Salad
Citrus Salad
Praline Chocolate Ice-cream Log
Tropical Fruit Pavlova Tower

Shrimp with Fresh Herb Dip

Preparation time:
30 minutes
Cooking time:
5 minutes
Serves 12

3 lb large cooked
  shrimp

Fresh Herb Dip
1 oz butter
2 green onions, chopped
2 garlic cloves, crushed
1 teaspoon sambal
  ulek
2 tablespoons chopped
  basil
2 tablespoons chopped
  parsley

2 tablespoons chopped
  mint
1 cup mayonnaise
1/2 cup heavy cream

1 Peel shrimp leaving
tails intact, devein.
Store in refrigerator
until required.
2 To make Dip: Melt
butter in small pan, add
green onions and garlic,
stir-fry over medium
heat until soft; cool.
Combine green onion
mixture in a medium
bowl with sambal
ulek, basil, parsley,
mint, mayonnaise
and cream.
3 Serve Fresh Herb Dip
with prepared shrimp.

◆ Unsuitable to freeze.

Clockwise from top: Glazed Leg of Ham (p. 5),
Shrimp with Fresh Herb Dip, Mushroom
and Thyme Pate (p. 4)

Mushroom and Thyme Pâté

Preparation time:
  15 minutes
Cooking time:
  12 minutes
Serves 12

2 oz butter
1 small onion,
  chopped
1 garlic clove,
  crushed
1 tablespoon thyme
  leaves

8 oz chicken livers,
  chopped
2 slices bacon,
  chopped
2 oz small mushroom
  caps
1/4 cup port
3/4 cup heavy cream

1 Melt butter in frying pan, add onion, garlic and thyme, stir-fry for 2 minutes or until onion is tender.
2 Add livers and bacon, stir-fry for 3 minutes or until browned. Add mushrooms and port, stir-fry 10 minutes or until most of the liquid has evaporated.
3 Place mixture into blender or food processor bowl, add cream, process to a smooth texture. Spoon into serving dish. Store, covered with plastic wrap, in refrigerator until needed.

Note: Pâté can be made up to 1 week ahead.
◆ Unsuitable to freeze.
◆ Serve with crackers or strips of raw vegetable.

1. *Glazed Leg of Ham. Remove rind gently with your hands.*

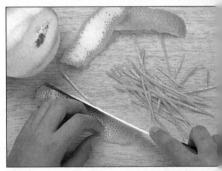

2. *Cut the rind of large orange into long, thin strips.*

3. *Add water, orange rind and cloves to baking dish.*

4. *Using a sharp knife, score the fat with deep cuts.*

Glazed Leg of Ham

Preparation time:
10 minutes
Cooking time:
3 hours 45 minutes
Serves 20

x 14 lb leg ham
large orange
cups water
whole cloves
1/4 cups light brown
sugar, firmly packed
tablespoon mustard
powder
cup orange
marmalade or
apricot jam
xtra whole cloves

Preheat oven to
moderate 350°F.
Remove rind from ham
by running a thumb
around the edge, under
the rind. Begin pulling
from the widest edge.
When rind has been
removed to within

4 inches of the shank
end, cut through the
rind around the shank.
Using a sharp knife,
remove excess fat from
ham; discard. Squeeze
juice from orange and
set aside.
2 Cut orange rind into
long, thin strips.
3 Place ham on a
roasting rack in deep
baking dish; add water,
peel and cloves to dish.
Cover ham and dish
securely with foil; cook
for 2 hours.
4 Remove from oven.
Drain meat and discard
pan juices. Using a sharp
knife, score the fat with
deep cuts crossways and
then diagonally to form
a diamond pattern.
5 Combine the sugar,
mustard and marmalade
in a medium bowl;
mix to a thick paste.
Spread half thickly
over the ham. Return
to a moderately hot
oven 415°F, and
cook, uncovered, for

about 30 minutes.
6 Combine orange juice
with remaining brown
sugar paste; stir until
smooth. Remove ham
from oven; brush with a
little brown sugar
mixture. Press a clove
into each diamond,
return to oven. Roast,
uncovered, for a further
hour; brush with the
brown sugar mixture
every 10 minutes.
Serve ham sliced,
warm or cold.

Note: Cover leftover
ham with a damp cloth;
store in refrigerator for
about 10 days. Change
cloth regularly.

5. *Combine the sugar, mustard and marmalade in a medium bowl.*

6. *Press a clove into each diamond, return ham to the oven.*

Chicken and Apricot Terrine

Preparation time:
1 hour
Cooking time:
1 hour 15 minutes
Serves 12

8 oz dried apricots
1/2 cup pine nuts
2 tablespoons oil
1 large onion,
   chopped
1 1/2 cups fresh white
   bread crumbs
1/3 cup chopped
   parsley
1 egg, lightly beaten
1 tablespoon oil,
   extra
1 oz butter
6 large boneless
   chicken breasts
1 tablespoon gelatin
1 cup light chicken
   stock

1 Preheat oven to moderate 350°F. You will need 2 loaf pans measuring 8 1/2 x 5 1/2 x 2 3/4 inches. Place apricots in medium bowl, pour over boiling water, stand for 10 minutes, drain, then chop apricots roughly using a sharp knife.
2 Place pine nuts in small dry pan, stir over medium heat until lightly golden; cool.
3 Heat oil in medium pan, add onion, stir-fry until soft, remove from heat, stir in apricots, pine nuts, bread crumbs, parsley and egg.
4 Heat extra oil and butter in a large pan, add chicken fillets. Cook over medium heat for about 4 minutes on each side or until almost cooked through. Remove from pan, drain on absorbent paper. Repeat with remaining chicken.
5 Using a sharp knife, carefully cut each fillet horizontally into 3 slices.
6. Arrange 1/4 chicken slices, browned side down, over base of one loaf pan. Spread with 1/3 of apricot mixture. Repeat layering using chicken slices and apricot mixture from one portion, ending with chicken, browned side up.
7 Cover terrine with aluminum foil and place into a shallow baking dish. Pour in enough boiling water to come halfway up sides of terrines. Bake for 1 hour 15 minutes or until firm; cool. Cover the dish with plastic wrap, then

Chicken and Apricot Terrine (left), Vegetable Slaw with Mustard Mayonnaise (page 8)

refrigerate until cold.
8 Turn terrine out, wash loaf pan, return terrine to pan. Combine gelatin with stock in a small bowl. Stand bowl in hot water, stir until gelatin dissolves. Spoon evenly over terrine, cover with plastic wrap, refrigerate until set. Turn terrine out of loaf pan, slice and serve.

Note: Terrines can be made up to 2 days ahead.
◆ Unsuitable to freeze.

Vegetable Slaw with Mustard Mayonnaise

Preparation time:
  20 minutes
Cooking time:
  Nil
Serves 12

3 cups finely sliced green cabbage
3 cups finely sliced red cabbage
2 red onions, finely sliced
3 large carrots, grated
3 large zucchini, grated

Mustard Dressing
1/2 cup mayonnaise
1/4 cup chopped parsley
3 garlic cloves, crushed
1 1/2 tablespoons whole-grain mustard

1 Layer green and red cabbage, onion, carrots and zucchini carefully

in serving bowl.
2 To make Mustard Dressing: Combine mayonnaise, parsley, garlic and mustard in small bowl.
3 Spoon Mustard Dressing over salad, store covered with plastic wrap in refrigerator. Toss Slaw just before serving.

Note: Slaw can be made a day ahead.
◆ Unsuitable to freeze.

Leafy Green Salad with Walnut Dressing

Preparation time:
  10 minutes
Cooking time:
  Nil
Serves 12

1 lb spinach
4 oz arugula (rocket)
1 small cos lettuce
2 cups snow pea shoots
1 1/2 cups flat-leafed Italian parsley

Dressing
1/2 cup olive oil
1/3 cup walnut oil
1/3 cup white wine vinegar
2 garlic cloves, crushed
2 teaspoons French mustard

1 Combine spinach, arugula, cos, shoots and parsley in a large bowl.

2 To make Dressing: Place oil, walnut oil, vinegar, garlic and mustard in a small jar. Shake for 20 seconds or until combined.
3 Add dressing to prepared salad, toss until combined.

Note: Arugula is a salad herb with a strong taste. You can grow it in temperate climates, or buy it in produce departments of some supermarkets. Snow pea shoots are usually sold in Asian markets. If these vegetables are not available, replace with other green salad vegetables and herbs.
◆ Unsuitable to freeze.

Wild and Brown Rice Salad

Preparation time:
  15 minutes
Cooking time:
  35 minutes
Serves 12

3 cups wild and brown rice mix
1/4 cup sesame oil
12 green onions, chopped
2 cobs corn, kernels removed
1 large bell pepper, seeded and chopped
1/2 cup chopped parsley

Dressing
3/4 cup oil

8

Clockwise from left: Citrus Salad (p. 10), Leafy Green Salad with Walnut Dressing, Wild and Brown Rice Salad

2 tablespoons white wine vinegar
1 tablespoon curry powder
1 tablespoon sugar
1 tablespoon grated ginger

1 Add rice mix to large pan of boiling water, simmer over medium heat for 30 minutes or until tender, drain, rinse under cold water.
2 Heat oil in medium pan, add green onion, corn kernels and bell pepper, stir-fry over medium heat 2 minutes or until tender.
3 Combine rice, vegetables and parsley in large mixing bowl.
4 To make Dressing: Place oil, vinegar, curry powder, sugar and ginger in a small jar. Shake vigorously for 20 seconds or until mixture is combined. Add dressing to salad, stir until all ingredients are combined.

Note: This salad can be made completely a day ahead. Cover with plastic wrap, store in refrigerator. Stir well just before serving. Wild and brown rice mix is available from supermarkets.
◆ Unsuitable to freeze.

Citrus Salad
Preparation time:
 20 minutes
Cooking time:
 Nil
Serves 12

2 large oranges
2 large grapefruit
2 large tangelos
12 radishes, sliced
1 Spanish onion, thinly
 sliced
1 English cucumber,
 sliced
1/2 cup cilantro leaves

Dressing
1/2 cup olive oil
2 tablespoons rice wine
 vinegar
3 teaspoons soy sauce
1 teaspoon sambal ulek

1 Peel rind and pith from oranges, grapefruit and tangelos, cut fruit into 1 1/4 inch slices, remove seeds.
2 Combine fruit slices in a large bowl with radish, onion, cucumber and cilantro.
3 To make Dressing: Place oil, vinegar, soy

sauce and sambal ulek in a small jar. Shake vigorously for 20 seconds or until combined. Pour over salad just before serving.

Note: Sambal ulek is a fiery mixture of crushed chilies and salt, available from supermarkets.
◆ Unsuitable to freeze.

Praline Chocolate Ice-cream Log
Preparation time:
 1 hour + freezing
Cooking time:
 Nil
Serves 12

Almond Praline
2/3 cup slivered almonds
2/3 cup sugar

Ice-cream mixture
1 cup dried mixed
 fruit
1/3 cup sweet sherry
16 cups vanilla ice-cream
2 x 6 1/2 oz rolls almond
 paste
6 1/2 oz dark chocolate,
 chopped
1 1/4 cups heavy cream,
 whipped

1 Line 2 loaf pans, 8 1/2 x 5 1/2 x 2 3/4 inches, smoothly with aluminum foil.
2 To make Almond

Praline: Scatter almonds on lightly oiled baking sheet, bake in moderate oven 350°F for 10 minutes or until lightly browned, cool on baking sheet. Place sugar in medium pan, heat gently without stirring until sugar begins to melt. Stir over low heat until evenly colored and sugar has been dissolved (soft-crack stage, 275°F on sugar thermometer). Remove from heat, pour evenly over almonds, allow to set, crush coarsely.
3 Combine mixed fruit and sherry in glass bowl, stand 2 hours. Soften one-third of the ice-cream, add crushed almond praline, reserving some larger pieces for decoration. Stir until combined. Divide mixture into loaf pans, freeze until firm.
4 Roll half of the almond paste into two rectangles large enough to cover ice-cream, return it to freezer.
5 Combine half remaining ice-cream and the chocolate in medium pan, stir over medium heat until chocolate has melted, pour into a bowl, freeze until semi-frozen. Divide between loaf pans, freeze until this

---

Praline Chocolate Ice-Cream Log (left), Tropical Fruit Pavlova Tower (p. 12)

layer is firm.
6 Roll remaining almond paste as above, place over chocolate layer, return to freezer.
7 Soften remaining ice-cream, add dried fruit mixture, stir until combined. Divide between loaf pans, freeze until firm.
8 **To serve:** Turn out onto serving plate, remove foil, pipe cream along the top of each log, sprinkle with the reserved almond praline.

Tropical Fruit Pavlova Tower

Preparation time:
  45 minutes
Cooking time:
  1 hour 30 minutes
Serves 12

cornstarch, for dusting
8 egg whites
2¹/2 cups sugar
8 oz cream cheese, softened
1 tablespoon lemon juice

¹/3 cup sugar, extra
1¹/4 cups heavy cream
1 small mango, puréed
1 lb sliced mixed fresh fruit

1 Preheat oven to very slow 250°F. Brush three baking sheets with melted butter or oil. Line each with waxed paper, grease paper. Dust lightly with sifted cornstarch, shake off excess. Using plates or cake pans as guides, mark a 9¹/2 inch circle on one baking sheet.

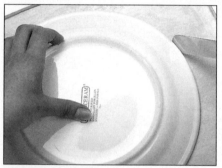

1. *Tropical Fruit Pavlova Tower. Mark circles on floured sheet with plate as guide.*

2. *Add sugar gradually to egg whites, beating constantly.*

3. *Pipe meringue into round shapes to the sizes marked on baking sheets.*

4. *Pipe about 20 small circles with leftover meringue.*

Mark a 7 inch, a 5 inch and a 2³/4 inch circle on another sheet. Leave remaining sheet unmarked.

2 Place egg whites in large, dry mixing bowl. Using electric beaters, beat egg whites until soft peaks form. Add sugar gradually, beating constantly until mixture is thick and glossy and all the sugar is dissolved.

3 Spoon mixture into a pastry bag fitted with a large plain tip and, using marked circles as guides, pipe meringue into 4 round shapes on prepared baking sheets.

4 Use leftover meringue to pipe about 20 small circles on remaining sheet. Bake for 1 hour 30 minutes or crisp, alternating shelf positions during cooking. Remove from oven, cool on baking sheets.

5 Using electric beaters, beat cream cheese, lemon juice and extra sugar in small mixing bowl until smooth. Beat cream in small bowl until soft peaks form, fold into cream cheese mixture with mango.

6 To assemble tower: Place large meringue layer on serving plate, spread with about 1 cup mango cream. Place 6 meringue circles around outside, about 1¹/4 inches in from the edge. Arrange some fruit around rosettes and in center. Top with 7 inch circle, spread with about ³/4 cup mango cream, 5 circles and more fruit. Continue layering as above, reducing the quantity of cream, rosettes and fruit as you go. Top the smallest meringue layer with mango cream, fruit and one rosette.

Note: Meringue layers can be made up to one week ahead and stored in airtight container.
◆ Assemble up to 4 hours ahead, store in refrigerator.
◆ Mango cream can be made a day ahead.
◆ Use any fruit of your choice, e.g. mangoes, cherries, nectarines, apricots, berries. Canned or frozen fruit may also be used.

HINT
Care needs to be taken storing meringues in a humid climate. If you are making them the day before serving, leave the cooked meringues in the oven without opening the door until you're ready to assemble them. A meringue that has softened can be crisped successfully in a slow oven.

5. Beat cream and fold into cream cheese mixture with mango.

6. Start assembling tower by spreading large meringue with mango cream.

Hot Dinner for 6

Avocado Salad with Lemon Mustard Sauce
Lemony Roast Turkey
Fluffy Potatoes
Baby Squash with Bacon
Asparagus Bean Bundles
Golden Steamed Pudding
Lemon Mascarpone Custard

Avocado Salad with Lemon Mustard Sauce

Preparation time:
  20 minutes
Cooking time:
  Nil
Serves 6

Lemon Mustard Sauce
1 tablespoon lemon juice
1 tablespoon tarragon
  vinegar
3 egg yolks
1 teaspoon French
  mustard
4 oz butter, melted

Salad
1 large carrot
3 green onions
2 avocados, sliced
1 mango, sliced
6 canned artichoke
  hearts, quartered
1/2 cup watercress leaves

1 To make Lemon Mustard Sauce:
Combine lemon juice, vinegar, egg yolks and mustard in a blender or food processor bowl. With motor constantly operating, add hot, bubbly butter in a thin steady stream, processing until all the butter is added. Transfer to small bowl, cover with plastic wrap.
2 Cut carrot and green onions into fine strips, about 1 1/2 inches long.
3 Spoon sauce onto serving plates, arrange carrot and green onion in the center. Top with avocado, mango and artichokes, garnish with watercress.

Clockwise from left: Avocado Salad with Lemon Mustard Sauce, Lemony Roast Turkey (p. 16) on platter with Asparagus Bean Bundles (p. 18) Baby Squash and Bacon (p. 17), and Fluffy Potatoes (p. 17)

14

1 Lemony Roast Turkey. Mix together stuffing ingredients.

2. Pat turkey dry, inside and out, with absorbent paper.

Lemony Roast Turkey

Preparation time:
  20 minutes
Cooking time:
  2 hours
Serves 6

Lemon Stuffing
3 cups fresh white bread crumbs
1 lb sausage meat
2 medium white onions, chopped
2 tablespoons chopped rosemary
2 garlic cloves, crushed
1/4 cup lemon juice
2 teaspoons grated lemon rind
1/2 cup slivered almonds

1 x 6 lb turkey
2 oz butter, melted
1 lemon, sliced
2 1/2 cups light chicken stock
1 1/2 cups white wine
2 tablespoons all-purpose flour

1/3 cup water
cranberry jelly, for serving

1 Preheat oven to moderately slow 315°F.
To make stuffing:
Combine bread crumbs in medium bowl with sausage meat, onions, rosemary, garlic, lemon juice, lemon rind and almonds. Discard turkey neck, pat turkey dry with absorbent paper. Spoon Lemon Stuffing into turkey, tie wings and drumsticks securely in place. Place on roasting rack over shallow baking dish, brush turkey with half the butter, lay lemon slices over breast. Pour stock and wine into baking dish. Cover turkey and dish with aluminum foil.
2 Bake for 1 hour 15 minutes. Remove foil and lemon slices, brush with remaining butter. Return to oven for 45 minutes. To test if turkey is cooked, pierce the thigh with a skewer. If juice runs clear, turkey is ready. If still pink, continue cooking for about 10 minutes. Remove from oven, leave, covered with foil, in a warm place for 10 minutes.
3 Strain pan juices, return to baking dish. Blend flour with water in small bowl or jug until smooth. Add to juices in pan, stir over medium heat for 2 minutes or until gravy boils and thickens, boil 2 minutes.
4 Remove string from turkey, carve, serve with stuffing, gravy and cranberry jelly.

Note: Stuffing can be made a day ahead.
◆ Unsuitable to freeze.
◆ Make sure frozen turkey is completely thawed before cooking.

16

3. Brush turkey with butter, lay lemon slices over breast.

4. Add blended flour and water to juices in the pan.

Baby Squash and Bacon

Preparation time:
 5 minutes
Cooking time:
 10 minutes
Serves 6

6¹/2 oz yellow baby squash
4 oz cherry tomatoes
3 slices bacon, finely chopped
2 oz butter
1 leek, sliced
1/4 cup chives cut into 1 inch lengths

1 Cut each squash in halves or, if larger, in quarters. Halve the cherry tomatoes.
2 Stir-fry bacon in small pan over medium heat for 2 minutes or until it is golden and crisp, drain on absorbent paper.
3 Heat butter in medium pan, add squash and leek, stir-fry over medium heat until tender. Add tomatoes, stir-fry until heated through but not mushy. Serve sprinkled with chopped bacon and chives.

Note: This recipe is best cooked just before serving.
◆ Unsuitable to freeze.

Fluffy Potatoes

Preparation time:
 15 minutes
Cooking time:
 20 minutes
Serves 8

3 medium boiling potatoes, chopped
3 medium carrots, chopped
1/4 cup sour cream
1/4 cup grated fresh Parmesan cheese
freshly ground black pepper

2 teaspoons sesame seeds
chili powder

1 Preheat oven to moderate 350°F. Brush a baking sheet with melted butter or oil. Cook potatoes and carrots in simmering water until tender, drain, mash with sour cream until light and fluffy, then add cheese and pepper.
2 Pile ¹/4 cup of mixture onto prepared baking sheet, use a fork to rough up the surface. Make similar size mounds with the rest of the mixture.
3 Sprinkle each mound with sesame seeds and a pinch of chili. Bake for 30 minutes or until lightly browned.

Note: This recipe can be prepared a day ahead, and baked just before serving.
◆ Unsuitable to freeze.

Asparagus Bean Bundles

Preparation time:
  10 minutes
Cooking time:
  5 minutes
Serves 6

10 oz asparagus
10 oz beans
6 long chives
3 oz butter

1 Cut asparagus in half. Trim both ends of beans to same length as asparagus.
2 Bring a medium pan of water to the boil, add asparagus, cook 2 minutes or until tender but not soft, lift out, rinse under cold water, drain. Repeat procedure with beans.
3 Gather asparagus and beans together in six bundles, wrap a chive around each bundle, tie carefully with a knot.
4 Melt butter in large pan, add bundles, cover, cook over medium heat for 3 minutes or until heated through, turn occasionally.

Note: Bundles can be prepared to end of Step 3 up to a day ahead. Store, covered with plastic wrap, in refrigerator, until time to cook.
◆ Unsuitable to freeze.

Golden Steamed Pudding

Preparation time:
  20 minutes
Cooking time:
  4 hours
Serves 6

6 oz butter
3/4 cup sugar
3 eggs
1/3 cup chopped glacé cherries
1/3 cup chopped glacé apricots
1/3 cup chopped glacé pineapple
1/4 cup chopped dried dates
1/4 cup golden raisins
1/4 cup mixed candied citrus peel
1/3 cup chopped walnuts
1 cup all-purpose flour
1/2 teaspoon baking soda

1 Brush an 8-cup capacity pudding basin or steamer with melted butter or oil. Line base with waxed paper, grease paper. Grease a large sheet of aluminum foil and a large sheet of waxed paper. Lay paper over foil, greased side up. Pleat both sheets in the center.
2 Using electric beaters, beat butter and sugar in small mixing bowl until light and creamy. Add eggs gradually, beating thoroughly after each addition.

3 Transfer mixture to larger mixing bowl, add fruits, walnuts and sifted dry ingredients, stir until combined.
4 Spoon mixture into prepared basin. Cover with the greased foil and paper, greased side down. Place lid over foil, bring clips up and secure with string. If you have no lid, lay a pleated dish towel over foil, tie it securely with string under the lip of the basin. Knot the four ends of the dish towel together to form a handle to lower the basin into the pan.
5 Place the basin on a trivet in a large, deep pan. Carefully pour boiling water down the side of the pan to come halfway up the side of the basin. Bring to the boil, cover, cook for 4 hours. Do not let the pudding boil dry, replenish with boiling water as the pudding cooks. Remove covering, invert pudding onto a plate. Serve with Lemon Mascarpone Custard.

Note: If not serving immediately, allow pudding to cool, store in refrigerator for up to 6 weeks. Reheat pudding by cooking the same way for 1 hour.
◆ Pudding can be frozen for up to 3 months.

Golden Steamed Pudding (left), Lemon Mascarpone Custard

Lemon Mascarpone Custard

Preparation time:
  5 minutes
Cooking time:
  5 minutes
Serves 6

2 tablespoons custard
  powder
1/3 cup sugar

1/2 cup orange juice
1 cup water
1/3 cup mascarpone
1/3 cup lemon butter
2 tablespoons Cointreau

1 Combine custard powder and sugar in pan, add orange juice and water, stir until combined. Stir over medium heat for 3 minutes, boil for a further 1 minute.
2 Add mascarpone, lemon butter and Cointreau, stir until heated through.

Note: Mascarpone is an Italian cream cheese. It is very rich and can be used as a substitute for cream. Available from delicatessens and large supermarkets.
◆ Custard powder can be bought in supermarkets selling import goods.
◆ Unsuitable to freeze.

19

Quick Menu for 8

Asparagus with Tangy Herb Sauce
Roast Turkey Breast with Parsley Crust
Scalloped Potatoes and Leek
Crunchy Apple Salad
Store-bought Christmas Pudding with Rum
Cream
Pistachio Orange Triangles

Asparagus with Tangy Herb Sauce

Preparation time:
  10 minutes
Cooking time:
  4 minutes
Serves 8

*6 x 8 oz bunches
  asparagus*
1/2 cup chopped chives

Tangy Herb Sauce
*1 cup watercress leaves,
  stalks removed*
1/2 cup mint leaves
1 1/4 cups sour cream
1/3 cup cream
*1 tablespoon lemon
  juice*

1 Add asparagus to a pan of boiling water, cook over high heat for 4 minutes or until tender but not mushy, drain.
2 To make Tangy Herb Sauce: Combine watercress and mint leaves in blender or food processor bowl, blend 1 minute or until finely chopped. Add sour cream, cream and lemon juice, blend 1 minute or until combined. Transfer mixture to medium pan, stir over medium heat for 3 minutes or until hot.
3 Divide asparagus into eight portions and serve each with a spoonful of Tangy Herb Sauce, sprinkled with chives.

Note: Sauce can be made a day ahead. Store, covered in plastic wrap, in refrigerator. Heat just before serving.
◆ Unsuitable to freeze.

Asparagus with Tangy Herb Sauce (at front), Roast Turkey Breast with Parsley Crust (p. 22)

Roast Turkey Breast with Parsley Crust

Preparation time:
 10 minutes
Cooking time:
 45 minutes
Serves 8

2 lb boneless turkey
 breast
1 egg, lightly beaten

Parsley Crust
2 oz butter
4 green onions, finely
 chopped
2 garlic cloves,
 crushed
2 cups fresh white
 bread crumbs
2 tablespoons finely
 chopped parsley

cranberry jelly, to
 serve

1 Preheat oven to
moderate 350°F.
Place turkey in deep
baking dish, pat dry
with absorbent paper.
Brush with egg.
**2 To make Parsley
Crust:** Melt butter
in small pan over
medium heat. Add
green onions and garlic,
stir until softened.
Add bread crumbs
and parsley, stir until
combined, cool.
3 Press Parsley Crust
firmly onto turkey.

Bake for 45 minutes
or until crust is
golden brown. Serve
turkey sliced, with
cranberry jelly.

Note: Crust can be
made a day ahead.
◆ Unsuitable to freeze.

Scalloped Potatoes and Leek

Preparation time:
 10 minutes
Cooking time:
 1 hour
Serves 8

6 medium (about 3 lb)
 floury potatoes,
 scrubbed and thinly
 sliced
4 leeks, sliced
freshly ground black
 pepper
2 teaspoons dried mixed
 herbs
2 cups chicken stock
1 oz butter

1 Preheat oven to
moderate 350°F.
Place potato and leek
slices in alternate
layers in a shallow
ovenproof dish,
sprinkle each layer
with pepper and herbs.
2 Pour over stock,
dot with butter,
cover loosely with
aluminum foil. Bake

for 1¹/2 hours or until
potatoes are tender.
◆ Unsuitable to freeze.

Crunchy Apple Salad

Preparation time:
 15 minutes
Cooking time:
 Nil
Serves 8

2 red apples
4 celery stalks
1 large red bell pepper
8 oz snow peas,
 trimmed both ends
¹/2 cup bottled French
 dressing
¹/2 cup roasted unsalted
 peanuts

1 Cut apples into
quarters, remove core,
slice thinly. Cut celery
stalks into straws
2¹/2 inches long.
Halve bell pepper,
remove seeds, cut into
2¹/2 inch straws.
2 In a large mixing
bowl combine apple,
celery, bell pepper and
snow peas. Add
dressing, toss well.
Serve salad sprinkled
with peanuts.

Note: Slice apples and
add dressing just before
serving.
◆ Unsuitable to freeze.

Scalloped Potatoes and Leek (left),
Crunchy Apple Salad

Store-bought Christmas Pudding with Rum Cream

Preparation time:
  5 minutes
Cooking time:
  Nil for Rum Cream;
  heating time for
  pudding

1 Christmas pudding

Rum Cream
4 oz cream cheese
2 oz butter, softened
1/3 cup confectioners'
  sugar
2 tablespoons dark rum
1 1/4 cups heavy cream

1 Reheat pudding following instructions on the packet.
2 To make Rum Cream: Using electric beaters, beat softened cream cheese, butter and confectioners' sugar until light and creamy. Add rum and cream, beat for 1 minute or until soft peaks form.
3 Serve heated pudding with Rum Cream.

Note: Rum Cream can be made 2 days ahead. Bring it to room temperature before serving.
◆ Unsuitable to freeze.

Pistachio Orange Triangles

Preparation time:
  15 minutes
Cooking time:
  Nil
Makes 36

1 cup Rice Krispies
8 oz plain, sweet
  cookies, crushed
1/2 cup shredded
  coconut
1/2 cup chopped
  pistachio nuts
4 oz butter, melted
1/2 cup condensed
  milk

Topping
4 oz cream cheese,
  softened
1/4 cup confectioners'
  sugar
2 teaspoons grated
  orange rind
2 tablespoons mixed
  peel, finely chopped
2 tablespoons pistachio
  nuts, extra, finely
  chopped

1 Brush a deep 11 1/2 x 7 1/2 x 1 1/4 inch jelly roll pan with melted butter or oil. Line base and sides with aluminum foil, grease foil.
2 Combine Rice Krispies, cookie crumbs, coconut and pistachio nuts in a large mixing bowl. Add butter and condensed milk, stir until combined.
3 Press mixture evenly into prepared pan, smooth surface, refrigerate until firm.
4 To make Topping: Combine cream cheese, confectioners' sugar and rind in a small bowl, stir until smooth. Spread over cookie base using a flat-bladed knife, sprinkle evenly with peel and nuts, cover with plastic wrap, refrigerate until firm. Lift out of pan, cut into triangles. Store in airtight container.

Note: This slice can be stored in refrigerator.
◆ Unsuitable to freeze.

> HINT
> You may like to skin the pistachio nuts. To do this, cover the shelled nuts with boiling water and let them stand two or three minutes. Drain and let cool slightly, then simply rub the skin off with your fingers while the nuts are still warm.

Store-bought Christmas Pudding with Rum Cream (at front), Pistachio Orange Triangles

Festive Lunch for 8

Pepper, Eggplant and Pesto Terrine
Roast Duck with Mandarin Sauce
Roasted Tomatoes with Herbs
Snap Pea and Fava Bean Salad
Festive Fruity Potatoes
Raspberry Mousse Cake

Pepper, Eggplant and Pesto Terrine

Preparation time:
  30 minutes
Cooking time:
  30 minutes
Serves 8

3 large red bell peppers
1 1/2 lb (about 2 small)
  eggplant
salt
1/3 cup oil
2 lb spinach
1/3 cup good-quality
  pesto

1 Preheat oven to moderate 350°F. Cut peppers in half, remove seeds. Place them cut side down on a baking sheet. Bake peppers for 30 minutes or until skin blisters and browns. Cool and peel. Drain well.
2 Cut eggplant into 1/4 inch slices, sprinkle with salt, stand 45 minutes. Rinse slices under cold water, drain, dry with absorbent paper.
3 Heat 1 tablespoon of the oil in pan, add a layer of eggplant slices. Cook over medium heat for 2 minutes on each side until lightly browned. Drain on absorbent paper. Repeat with remaining oil and eggplant. Cool and drain.
4 Remove stalks from spinach, place leaves in medium bowl, cover with hot water, stand 10 seconds, drain, rinse under cold water. Line a 12 1/2 x 5 inch terrine or pâté mold with a double layer of spinach leaves, allowing leaves to drape over sides of pan.
5 Place a quarter of the eggplant in overlapping slices along the base of pan. Top with a third of the pepper, spread with a quarter of the pesto. Repeat layering

Clockwise from left: Pepper, Eggplant and Pesto Terrine, Roast Duck with Mandarin Sauce (p. 28), Roasted Tomatoes with Herbs (p. 29)

with remaining eggplant, pepper and pesto.
6 Enclose filling completely with spinach leaves. Bake for 45 minutes or until tender, set aside to cool. Store terrine, covered with plastic wrap, in refrigerator. Turn out, serve sliced.

Note: Terrine can be made up to 2 days ahead.
◆ Unsuitable to freeze.
◆ Terrine and pâté

molds are available from specialty kitchenware stores. If unavailable, use a loaf pan.
◆ Pesto is available in jars from supermarkets, delicatessens and pasta shops, or you can make your own.

Roast Duck with Mandarin Sauce

Preparation time:
  30 minutes
Cooking time:
  1 hour 40 minutes
Serves 8

3 x 3 lb ducks
2 oz butter, melted

Stuffing
3 oz butter
12 green onions,
  chopped

1. Roast Duck with Mandarin Sauce. Stir-fry vegetables, add bread crumbs.

2. Spoon Stuffing into ducks, dividing it equally between each.

3. Tie wings and drumsticks of each duck securely in place.

4. For Sauce, blend cornstarch and stock, add remaining ingredients.

3 garlic cloves, crushed
3 teaspoons grated
  ginger
8 cups (about 1 lb) fresh
  white bread crumbs
1/4 cup chopped fresh
  cilantro
2 eggs, lightly beaten

Mandarin Sauce
1 x 10 oz can
  mandarin segments
2 tablespoons
  cornstarch
4 cups light chicken
  stock
1/2 cup orange juice
2 tablespoons lemon
  juice
1 tablespoon honey
1 tablespoon soy sauce
2 teaspoons grated
  ginger
1 tablespoon sugar

1 Preheat oven to
moderate 350°F. Rinse
ducks, pat dry with
absorbent paper.
2 To make Stuffing:
Heat butter in medium
pan, add green onions,
garlic and ginger, stir-fry

for 3 minutes or until
soft, add bread crumbs,
cilantro and eggs, stir
until combined. Remove
from heat.
3 Spoon Stuffing into
ducks, ensuring each
has the same amount.
4 Tie wings and
drumsticks securely
in place. Place ducks
on roasting rack over
shallow baking dish,
brush with butter.
Roast for 1 hour, baste
ducks occasionally
with pan juices.
5 While ducks are
roasting, prepare
Mandarin Sauce.
Process undrained
mandarins to a smooth
texture in blender or
food processor. Place
cornstarch in small
pan, add a little stock,
stir until smooth. Add
remaining stock,
orange and lemon juice,
honey, soy sauce, ginger,
sugar and mandarin
purée. Stir over
medium heat until

sauce boils and thickens.
6 Remove ducks from
oven, drain pan juices,
place ducks in baking
dish, pour over
Mandarin Sauce. Roast
further 40 minutes. To
test if duck is cooked,
insert skewer into the
thigh. If juice runs clear,
duck is ready. Strain
sauce, serve with ducks.
◆ Unsuitable to freeze.

Roasted Tomatoes with Herbs

Preparation time:
  15 minutes
Cooking time:
  20 minutes
Serves 8

4 medium ripe
  tomatoes
2 teaspoons thyme
  leaves
sugar
salt
freshly ground black
  pepper

5. Pour Mandarin Sauce over ducks, roast
further 40 minutes.

6. Insert a skewer in thigh; if juices run
clear, duck is cooked.

29

Dressing
2 tablespoons olive oil
4 green onions, finely
  chopped
2 garlic cloves, crushed
1 tablespoon balsamic
  vinegar
2 tablespoons shredded
  basil leaves

1 Preheat oven to
moderate 350°F.
Brush a baking sheet
with melted butter or
oil. Place tomatoes in
medium bowl, cover
with boiling water,
stand 1 minute, drain,
rinse under cold water.
Peel tomatoes, cut
horizontally in half,
scoop out seeds.
2 Place tomatoes, cut
side up, on prepared
baking sheet, sprinkle
with thyme, sugar, salt
and pepper. Bake for
20 minutes or until
tomatoes are tender
but not mushy; cool.
3 To make Dressing:
Heat oil in small pan,
add green onions and
garlic, stir-fry over
medium heat until soft,
cool, stir in vinegar.
4 Serve tomatoes cut
side down, spoon over
dressing, sprinkle with
shredded basil.

Note: Serve tomatoes at
room temperature; they
can be cooked up to
4 hours ahead. Spoon
dressing over just before
serving.
◆ Unsuitable to freeze.

30

Snap Pea and Fava Bean Salad

Preparation time:
  15 minutes
Cooking time:
  Nil
Serves 8

1 lb shelled fava beans
8 oz snap (sugar) peas
1/2 cup olive oil
4 leeks, sliced
4 garlic cloves, crushed
1 tablespoon French
  mustard
1 tablespoon balsamic
  vinegar
2 teaspoons sambal ulek
  or 1 small red chili,
  finely chopped

1 Bring a pan of water
to boil, add fava beans
and snap peas, simmer
for 2 minutes or until
just tender, drain, rinse
under cold water.
2 Heat oil in small pan,
add leeks and garlic,
stir-fry over high heat
2 minutes or until soft.
Remove from heat,
cool. Stir in mustard,
vinegar and sambal
ulek, add to fava beans
and peas, stir until
combined.

Note: Salad can be
prepared up to 4 hours
ahead. Stir well just
before serving.

Festive Fruity Potatoes

Preparation time:
  20 minutes
Cooking time:
  45 minutes
Serves 8

4 medium new potatoes
  (about 2 lb)
2 lb orange sweet
  potato
3/4 cup dried apricots
3/4 cup raisins
2/3 cup orange juice
2 oz butter
2 tablespoons chopped
  chives

1 Preheat oven to
moderate 350°F. Cut
potato and sweet potato
into 1 1/4 inch cubes.
Cook in simmering water
for 5 minutes, drain.
2 Combine apricots,
raisins and orange juice
in small pan, cover, bring
to boil, remove from
heat, stand 5 minutes.
3 Combine potatoes
and undrained fruit in
a shallow ovenproof
dish, dot with butter.
Bake for 45 minutes or
until lightly browned.
Stir occasionally.
Garnish with chives.

Note: This dish can be
prepared up to baking
stage 4 hours ahead.

*Snap Pea and Fava Bean Salad (top),
Fruity Potatoes*

Raspberry Mousse Cake

Preparation time:
45 minutes
Cooking time:
15 minutes
Serves 8

Cake
2 tablespoons
all-purpose flour
2 tablespoons
self-rising flour
2 tablespoons
cornstarch
2 eggs
1/3 cup sugar

Raspberry Mousse
13 oz fresh or frozen
raspberries
1 egg, extra
1/3 cup sugar, extra
8 oz packet cream
cheese, softened
1 1/4 cups heavy
cream
1 tablespoon gelatin
2 tablespoons
water

To Serve
confectioners' sugar

1 Preheat oven to moderate 350°F. Brush an 8 inch round springform pan with melted butter or oil. Line base and sides with waxed paper; grease paper.
To make Cake: Sift flours and cornstarch 3 times onto waxed paper.
2 Using electric beaters, beat eggs in small mixing bowl for 3 minutes or until thick and pale.
3 Add sugar gradually, beating constantly until dissolved and mixture is pale yellow and glossy. Transfer mixture to large mixing bowl.
4 Using a metal spoon, fold in dry ingredients quickly and lightly.
5 Spread mixture evenly into prepared pan. Bake for 15 minutes or until sponge is lightly golden

and shrinks from side of pan. Leave sponge in the pan for 3 minutes before turning out onto wire rack to cool.
6 To make Raspberry Mousse: Process 10 oz raspberries to a smooth texture in blender or food processor bowl, pass through a fine sieve. Reserve half of the purée for serving.
7 Using electric beaters, beat extra egg and extra sugar in a small bowl until creamy. Add cream cheese, beat until smooth. In a separate bowl beat cream until soft peaks form.
8 Combine gelatin with water in small bowl, stand bowl in hot water, stir until gelatin dissolves.
9 Using a metal spoon fold gelatin, half raspberry purée and reserved whole raspberries into cream

1. *Raspberry Mousse Cake. Beat sugar into eggs until pale and glossy.*

2. *Spread cake mixture evenly into prepared pan.*

Raspberry Mousse Cake

cheese mixture, then fold in cream. Cover with plastic wrap and refrigerate for 10 minutes or until mixture has thickened, stirring occasionally.
10 To assemble: Cut cake in half horizontally. Place first cake layer back in clean, lined pan. Spread cake evenly with mousse. Top with remaining cake layer, refrigerate until the mousse has set.
11 To serve: Sift confectioners' sugar over top of cake, cut into wedges. Place onto serving plates and spoon reserved purée around cake.
Note: Cake can be made a day ahead. Store, covered in plastic wrap, in refrigerator.
◆ Unsuitable to freeze.

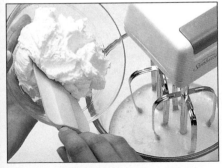

3. Add cream cheese to mousse mixture, beat until smooth.

4. Fold gelatin, half purée and whole raspberries into cream cheese mixture.

33

Gifts and Cakes

S ome of the most welcome Christmas gifts are homemade and edible. The cookies, chocolates, candies and cakes in this chapter make delightful presents. Put them in a jar, tin or box, wrap them in pretty paper and remember to enclose heating or storage instructions if applicable.

Apple Mincemeat Tarts

Preparation time:
  30 minutes
Cooking time:
  15 minutes
Makes about 24

1 1/2 *cups all-purpose*
  flour
1/2 *cup self-rising flour*
4 *oz butter, chopped*
2 *teaspoons grated*
  lemon rind
1/4 *cup water*

Filling
1 *small green apple,*
  cored, peeled
13 *oz jar mincemeat*
sugar for sprinkling

1 Preheat oven to moderately hot 415°F. Brush shallow muffin pans with melted butter or oil. Sift all-purpose and self-rising flours into mixing bowl, add chopped butter and lemon rind. Using fingertips, rub butter into flour until mixture is a fine, crumbly texture. Add almost all the water, mix to a soft dough, adding more water if necessary. Turn onto lightly floured surface, knead 1 minute or until smooth. Remove one-third pastry, cover with plastic wrap, place in freezer. Cover remaining pastry with plastic wrap, refrigerate for 10 minutes.
2 Roll large portion of pastry out thinly. Cut into circles using a fluted 2 3/4 inch round cutter, press circles into prepared pans. Gather pastry scraps together, roll out and cut into

Clockwise from left: Apple Mincemeat Tarts, Liqueur Cream Sauce (p. 37), Panettone (p. 37), Apricot Chocolate Truffles (p. 36)

circles, as before. Add any leftover scraps to pastry in freezer.

3 To make filling: Grate apple coarsely, drain on absorbent paper. Combine apple and mincemeat. Place tablespoons of mixture into pastry cases. Coarsely grate frozen pastry, sprinkle over tarts. Sprinkle with sugar.

4 Bake for 15 minutes or until lightly browned, cool on racks.

Note: Store tarts in an airtight container for up to 2 weeks.
◆ Tarts can be frozen for up to 3 months.

HINT
Grated frozen pastry sprinkled with sugar makes a crisp topping for any sweet pie.

Apricot Chocolate Truffles

Preparation time:
  30 minutes
Cooking time:
  Nil
Makes about 25

1 cup Rice Krispies
1/2 cup shredded coconut
1/4 cup chopped dried
  apricots
1/4 cup chopped mixed
  peel
1/4 cup slivered almonds
3/4 cup sweetened
  condensed milk
8 oz white chocolate,
  chopped
3 1/2 oz dark chocolate,
  chopped
2 teaspoons white
  vegetable shortening

1 In a medium mixing bowl, combine Rice Krispies, coconut, apricots, peel and almonds. Add condensed milk, stir

until combined, cover with plastic wrap, refrigerate until firm.

2 Shape heaped teaspoons of mixture into balls.

3 Place white chocolate in small heatproof bowl. Stand bowl over pan of simmering water, stir until chocolate has melted and is smooth. Place a wire rack over a baking sheet. Using two forks, dip truffles into chocolate, allow excess to run off, place onto wire rack, refrigerate until set.

4 Melt dark chocolate and white vegetable shortening as for Step 3, spoon over tops of truffles, allowing it to drizzle down sides. Refrigerate until set.

Note: Truffles can be decorated with chopped glace cherries, toasted slivered almonds or miniature holly leaves.
◆ Unsuitable to freeze.

1. Apricot Chocolate Truffles. Mix together ingredients for center of truffles.

2. Shape heaped teaspoons of mixture into balls.

Liqueur Cream Sauce

Preparation time:
  10 minutes
Cooking time:
  5 minutes
Makes 3 cups

3 oz butter
1 cup sugar
6 egg yolks
1/2 cup sweet sherry
1/2 cup brandy
1 1/4 cups heavy cream

1 Using electric beaters, beat butter and sugar in medium heatproof bowl. Add egg yolks, sherry, brandy and cream, beat until well combined.
2 Place bowl over pan of simmering water, stir 5 minutes or until mixture thickens slightly and coats the back of a wooden spoon with a creamy layer. Do not boil.

Note: Liqueur Cream Sauce can be stored in the refrigerator for up to 1 week.
◆ Unsuitable to freeze.

Panettone

Preparation time:
  1 hour 30 minutes
Cooking time:
  1 hour 15 minutes
Makes one 8 inch loaf

3/4 cup mixed fruit
2 tablespoons mixed candied citrus peel
2 tablespoons orange juice
1 1/2 oz fresh yeast
1 teaspoon sugar
2 tablespoons lukewarm water
3 cups all-purpose flour
2 oz butter
3 eggs, lightly beaten
2 tablespoons sugar
1/2 cup lukewarm milk
extra milk for glazing

1 Preheat oven to moderately hot 415°F.

Brush an 8 inch charlotte tin with melted butter or oil. Combine mixed fruit, peel and orange juice in a small bowl, let stand while preparing rest of cake.
2 Combine yeast, sugar and water in a medium mixing bowl, blend until smooth. Stand bowl, covered with plastic wrap, in warm place for about 10 minutes or until foamy.
3 Sift flour into large mixing bowl, add butter. Using fingertips, rub butter into flour for 2 minutes or until mixture is a fine, crumbly texture. Add fruit mixture, stir until well mixed.
4 Combine eggs, sugar and milk, stir in yeast mixture. Make a well in center of flour, add yeast mixture. Using a knife, mix to a soft, wet dough.
5 Using your hand, vigorously beat dough

3. Using two forks, dip truffles into white chocolate.

4. Spoon melted dark chocolate over tops of truffles, letting it drizzle down sides.

for 5 minutes or until dough becomes slightly stringy, smooth and glossy. Scrape mixture down side of bowl. Leave, covered with plastic wrap, in warm place for 30 minutes or until well risen.
6 Repeat beating procedure for further 5 minutes, turn dough onto lightly floured surface, knead for 10 minutes, or until dough is no longer sticky. Place into prepared pan, leave, covered with plastic wrap, in warm place for about 30 minutes or until well risen.
7 Brush with extra milk, bake for 15 minutes, reduce heat to moderate, 350°F, bake further 1 hour or until well-browned and cooked through. When cooked, panettone will sound hollow when tapped. Turn onto wire rack to cool.

Note: If you don't have a charlotte tin, use an 8-cup pudding basin or an 8 inch round cake pan.
♦ Panettone is best eaten on day of baking, but it will stay fresh for up to 4 days, covered in plastic wrap.
♦ Can be frozen for up to 2 months.

Cherry Chocolates

Preparation time:
  30 minutes
Cooking time:
  Nil
Makes about 40

4 oz unsalted butter
2 cups confectioners' sugar
1/3 cup heavy cream
2 cups shredded coconut
pink food coloring
6 1/2 oz glacé cherries
3 1/2 oz dark chocolate, chopped
1 oz white vegetable shortening
2 oz white cooking chocolate

1 Heat butter in small pan until lightly browned, remove from heat. Add sifted confectioners' sugar, cream, coconut and a few drops of food coloring, stir until combined.
2 Take about 2 teaspoons of mixture and press evenly around each cherry.
3 Place dark chocolate and shortening in small heatproof bowl. Stand bowl over pan of simmering water, stir until the chocolate and shortening have melted and mixture is smooth.

4 Place a wire rack over a baking sheet. Using two forks, dip cherries into chocolate, allow excess to run off, place cherries onto wire rack, allow to set.
5 Place white chocolate in small heatproof bowl. Stand bowl over pan of simmering water, stir until chocolate has melted. Cool slightly and spoon into a small paper pastry bag. Seal open end. Snip tip off bag, drizzle white chocolate decoratively over cherry chocolates, allow to set.

Note: Cherry Chocolates can be refrigerated in an airtight container for up to 2 weeks.

HINTS

An easy pastry bag can be made by spooning mixture into the corner of a small plastic bag. Twist the open end to seal it and snip off corner of bag.
♦ ♦ ♦
Chocolate may also be melted in the microwave. It takes only a very few seconds; however, too long and it will burn. Microwave-melted chocolate doesn't look melted until you stir it.

Clockwise from left: Cherry Chocolates, Gingerbread Christmas Tree (p. 40), Apricot & Lemon Jam (p. 41)

Gingerbread Christmas Tree

Preparation time:
 1 hour
Cooking time:
 15 minutes
Makes 1 tree about
 10 inches high

4 oz butter
1/2 cup sugar
1 egg yolk
1/4 cup honey
2 cups all-purpose
 flour

1 teaspoon baking soda
2 teaspoons ground
 ginger
mixed color decorator
 balls
1 egg white
1 1/2 cups confectioners'
 sugar, approximately
5 ice-cream cones
confectioners' sugar
 for dusting

1 Preheat oven to moderate 350°F. Brush baking sheets with melted butter or oil. Using electric beaters, beat butter and sugar in small mixing bowl until light and creamy. Add egg yolk and honey, beat until combined.
2 Add sifted flour, baking soda and ginger, press together to form a soft dough. Turn onto lightly floured surface, knead 1 minute until smooth. Leave, covered with plastic wrap, in refrigerator 15 minutes.
3 Roll dough out to about 1/4 inch thick, between two sheets of waxed paper. Cut 30 Christmas tree

1. *Gingerbread Christmas Tree. Add egg yolk and honey to creamed mixture.*

2. *Cut six star shapes from the remaining dough, using a 1 1/2 inch cutter.*

3. *Press a decorator ball onto the top of each tree and onto one point of each star.*

4. *Add sifted confectioners' sugar to egg white, 1 tablespoon at a time.*

shapes from the dough using a 3 inch cutter. Re-roll the dough scraps and re-use. Cut six star shapes from the remaining dough, using a 1^{1}/2 inch cutter. Place on prepared baking sheets, allowing room to spread. Press decorator balls onto the top of each tree and onto one point of each star. Bake for 15 minutes or until lightly golden, cool on wire rack.
4 Using electric beaters, beat egg white until slightly frothy. Add sifted confectioners' sugar, 1 tablespoon at a time, beating until smooth between additions. Add enough confectioners' sugar to give a stiff spreading consistency.
5 To assemble tree: Stack cones on top of each other, spreading a little icing between each to join them together. Starting with the bottom cone, spread icing thickly. Press Christmas tree and

star cookies into the icing, stacking cookies in overlapping layers around the cone. Work your way up the cones in this manner, spreading with icing as you go. Leave room at the top, spread with icing. Press two stars, standing upright back to back, on the top. Sift extra confectioners' sugar over tree.

Note: If cookies won't adhere to cones, add more sifted confectioners' sugar to icing to give a stiffer consistency.
◆ Cookies can be made up to 2 days ahead; store in an airtight container. Once assembled, cover tree with plastic wrap until serving time.
◆ Unsuitable to freeze.

Apricot and Lemon Jam

Preparation time:
  15 minutes
Cooking time:
  1 hour
Makes about 3 cups

1 lb dried apricots
9 cups water
5 lemons
8 cups sugar

1 Soak apricots in half the water overnight. Boil whole lemons, uncovered, in remaining water until soft. Remove lemons and retain water. When cold, slice lemons thinly, removing pips and setting aside.
2 Boil apricots in their soaking water until tender, add sugar and sliced lemons, together with the reserved water and pips. (Tie the pips in a small muslin square.)

5. Stack cones on top of each other, spreading a little icing between.

6. Press Christmas tree cookies into the icing.

Boil until the jam thickens and a teaspoon of the mixture placed on a saucer wrinkles when it is pushed with your finger.
3 Remove pips and spoon jam into sterilized jars. Seal while still hot.

Crispy Milk Truffles

Preparation time:
  10 minutes
Cooking time:
  Nil
Makes about 24

8 oz milk chocolate,
  roughly chopped
few drops peppermint
  extract
1¹/2 cups fried
  unflavored egg
  noodles

1 Cover a baking sheet with a sheet of waxed paper. Place chocolate in a medium heatproof bowl. Stand over pan of simmering water, stir until chocolate has melted and mixture is smooth, remove it from heat.
2 Add peppermint extract and noodles, stir until combined.
3 Place heaped teaspoons of mixture onto prepared baking sheet, refrigerate until set.

Note: Noodles are available from supermarkets and Asian food stores.

Note: Either dark or white chocolate can be used instead of milk chocolate, if you prefer.
◆ Unsuitable to freeze.
◆ Truffles can be stored in an airtight container in refrigerator for up to 2 weeks.

Rocky Road

Preparation time:
  30 minutes
Cooking time:
  20 minutes
Makes about 25 pieces

2 tablespoons gelatin
1¹/2 cups water
2 cups sugar
pink food coloring
¹/2 cup unsalted roasted
  peanuts
¹/3 cup chopped glacé
  cherries
³/4 cup shredded coconut
1 lb milk chocolate,
  roughly chopped

1 Cover a baking sheet with a sheet of waxed paper. Sprinkle gelatin over ¹/2 cup of the water, stir until combined. Combine remaining water and sugar in a medium pan, stir over medium heat without boiling until sugar has completely dissolved. Bring to the boil, reduce heat to low, add gelatin mixture stir until combined, cook uncovered for 10 minutes, cool mixture to lukewarm.
2 Pour mixture into a large mixing bowl. Using electric beaters, beat on high speed for 8 minutes or until mixture is white and very thick.
3 Pour half of the mixture into a loaf pan. Add a few drops of food coloring to remaining mixture, stir until combined, pour into another loaf pan. Refrigerate both mixtures until set. Turn out, cut into 1¹/4 inch cubes.
4 In a large mixing bowl, combine the cubes of marshmallow, the peanuts, cherries and coconut.
5 Place chocolate in a medium heatproof bowl. Stand bowl over pan of simmering water, stir until chocolate has melted and the mixture is smooth. Add to marshmallow mixture. Stir until well combined, spoon onto prepared baking sheet, refrigerate until set. Cut into bite-size pieces.

Note: For ease of melting and mixing, use milk cooking chocolate.
◆ Can be stored, covered in plastic wrap, in refrigerator for up to 2 weeks.
◆ Unsuitable to freeze.

Clockwise from left: Crispy Milk Truffles, Mandarin and Passion Fruit Butter, Rocky Road

Mandarin and Passion Fruit Butter

Preparation time:
  5 minutes
Cooking time:
  6 minutes
Makes 2 cups

4 eggs, lightly beaten
2/3 cup sugar
1/3 cup passion fruit pulp
3 tablespoons mandarin
  juice
4 oz unsalted butter,
  roughly chopped

1 Combine eggs, sugar, passion fruit pulp, mandarin juice and butter in a medium heatproof bowl.
2 Place bowl over pan of simmering water, stir constantly for about 6 minutes or until mixture thickens slightly and thinly coats the back of a wooden spoon. Pour into hot, sterilized jars, seal while hot.

Note: Do not allow mixture to boil as curdling will result.
◆ Store in refrigerator for up to 3 weeks.

43

Chocolate Super Cookies

Preparation time:
  15 minutes
Cooking time:
  10 minutes
Makes about 30

4 oz butter
3¹/2 oz dark chocolate,
  roughly chopped
1 cup brown sugar
2 eggs, lightly beaten
1 cup all-purpose flour
¹/2 cup cocoa powder
¹/2 cup roughly chopped
  unsalted, roasted
  macadamia nuts
¹/3 cup golden raisins
3¹/2 oz white chocolate,
  roughly chopped
3¹/2 oz milk chocolate,
  roughly chopped

1 Preheat oven to
moderately hot 415°F.
Brush baking sheets
with melted butter or
oil. Melt butter in
small pan, add dark
chocolate, stir over
low heat until melted.
Transfer to large bowl.
2 Add sugar and eggs,
stir until combined. Add
sifted flour and cocoa,
nuts, golden raisins, white
and milk chocolate, stir
until combined.
3 Drop tablespoons of
mixture onto prepared
baking sheet, allowing
room for spreading.
Bake for 10 minutes or
until just set. Transfer
to wire rack to cool.

Note: Store cookies in
an airtight container for
up to 1 week.
◆ Can be frozen for
up to 2 months.

Chili Cheese Crackers

Preparation time:
  15 minutes
Cooking time:
  15 minutes
Makes about 25

1 cup all-purpose
  flour
¹/4 cup self-rising
  flour
2 teaspoons dry
  mustard powder
¹/2 teaspoon chili
  powder
4 oz butter, chopped
¹/2 cup grated
  Parmesan cheese
¹/4 cup water
milk, for glazing
1 tablespoon sesame
  seeds

1 Preheat oven to
moderate 350°F. Brush
baking sheets with
melted butter or oil. Sift
all-purpose and self-
rising flours, mustard
and chili into a large
mixing bowl, add
chopped butter. Using
fingertips, rub butter
into flour for 2 minutes
or until mixture is a fine,
crumbly texture, stir in
cheese. Add almost all
the water, mix to a soft
dough, adding more
water if necessary.
2 Turn onto lightly
floured surface, knead
for 1 minute or until
smooth, shape dough
into a log, 2 inches in
diameter. Store, covered
with plastic wrap, in
refrigerator, 15 minutes.
Using a sharp knife, cut
log into 1¹/4 inch-thick
circles. Place on prepared
baking sheets, allowing
room for spreading.
3 Brush circles with
milk, sprinkle with
sesame seeds. Bake for
15 minutes or until
lightly golden, loosen,
cool on baking sheets
5 minutes, transfer
to wire rack to cool
completely.

Note: Store crackers
in an airtight container
for up to 1 week.
◆ Can be frozen for up
to 2 months.

HINT
Chili Cheese Crackers
are delicious served
with cheese and pâté.
This combination of
goodies would make
a great gift from the
kitchen.

Chocolate Super Cookies (top), Chili Cheese
Crackers

Lemon and Almond Shortbread Wedges

Preparation time:
  15 minutes
Cooking time:
  40 minutes
Makes 12 wedges

8 oz butter
1/3 cup sugar
2 teaspoons grated
  lemon rind
1³/4 cups all-purpose
  flour
1³/4 cups rice flour
1/2 cup ground almonds
sugar for sprinkling

1 Preheat oven to
moderately slow 315°F.
Brush a baking sheet
with melted butter or
oil. Using electric
beaters, beat butter,
sugar and lemon rind
until light and creamy.
2 Add sifted all-purpose
and rice flour and
almonds, press together
to form a soft dough.
Turn onto a lightly
floured surface, knead
5 minutes.
3 Roll dough into a
9 inch circle using a
cake pan as a guide,
place onto greased
baking sheet.
4 Pinch a frill around
the edge of the circle.
Use a large knife to
score into 12 wedges.
Prick evenly with a fork,

sprinkle with sugar. Bake
for 40 minutes or until
lightly golden. Cut again,
cool on baking sheet.

Note: Store in an
airtight container for
up to 1 month.
♦ Shortbread can be
frozen for up to
3 months.

Beetroot and Ginger Relish

Preparation time:
  15 minutes
Cooking time:
  1 hour 10 minutes
Makes about 4 cups

6 medium beetroot
  (2 lb)
1 cup sugar
2 cups white wine
  vinegar
1 onion, chopped
1 green bell pepper,
  chopped
2 green apples, peeled,
  chopped
2 teaspoons grated fresh
  ginger
1 tablespoon whole-
  grain mustard

1 Place whole, unpeeled
beetroot in a large pan,
cover with water, bring
to boil, cover, reduce
heat to low, cook
45 minutes or until
beetroot is tender, drain.
Peel beetroot, cut into
1/2 inch cubes.
2 Combine sugar, vinegar,

onion, bell pepper, apple,
ginger and mustard in
large pan, bring to boil,
reduce heat to low, cook
uncovered for 15 minutes
or until reduced by half.
3 Add beetroot, cook
10 minutes. Spoon into
hot, sterilized jars, seal
while hot.

Note: Store relish in
refrigerator for up to
1 month.
♦ Unsuitable to freeze.

Curry Paste

Preparation time:
  10 minutes
Cooking time:
  6 minutes
Makes 1 cup

2 tablespoons oil
1 onion, finely chopped
2 cloves garlic, crushed
2 teaspoons grated ginger
2 tablespoons ground
  coriander
1 tablespoon ground
  cumin
1 tablespoon dry
  mustard powder
1 tablespoon ground
  turmeric
1 tablespoon ground
  cinnamon
2 teaspoons chili sauce
1/3 cup oil, extra
2 tablespoons vinegar
2 tablespoons lemon
  juice

1 Heat oil in a small
pan, add onion, garlic

Clockwise from left: Beetroot and Ginger Relish, Curry Paste, Lemon and Almond Shortbread Wedges.

and ginger, stir over low heat until onion is soft.
2 Add coriander, cumin, mustard, turmeric and cinnamon, stir over low heat 2 minutes. Add chili sauce, extra oil, vinegar and lemon juice, stir over medium heat for 3 minutes or until mixture thickens. Cool. Spoon into a sterilized jar, seal.

Note: Include a simple curry recipe (see right) with your gift.

Quick Chicken Curry

Serves 4
1 tablespoon oil
1 onion, cut into eighths
6 boneless chicken thighs, cut into strips
1/2 cup curry paste
1/2 cup coconut milk
2 tablespoons chopped fresh cilantro

1 Heat oil in a frying pan, add onion, stir-fry over high heat for 2 minutes.
2 Add chicken, stir-fry over high heat until browned. Add curry paste, stir-fry over high heat for 1 minute.
3 Add coconut milk, simmer uncovered for 10 minutes or until chicken is cooked and sauce thickened. Stir in cilantro.

47

Caramel Nut Tarts

Preparation time:
25 minutes
Cooking time:
15 minutes
Makes 24

1¹/2 cups all-purpose
flour
2 tablespoons cornstarch
4 oz butter, chopped
2 tablespoons water
1¹/3 cups sugar
4 tablespoons water,
extra
2/3 cup cream
1¹/2 cups roasted,
unsalted mixed
nuts

1 Preheat oven to
moderately hot 415°F.
Brush shallow muffin
pans with melted butter
or oil. Sift flour and
cornstarch into large
mixing bowl, add
chopped butter. Using
fingertips, rub butter
into flour for 2 minutes
or until mixture is a fine
crumbly texture. Add
water, mix until
combined. Turn onto a
lightly floured surface,
knead 1 minute or until
smooth. Store, covered
with plastic wrap, in
refrigerator 10 minutes.
2 Roll pastry out
thinly. Cut into circles
using a 2³/4 inch
round cutter, press
circles into prepared
pans. Prick pastry

evenly with a fork. Bake
10 minutes or until
lightly golden; cool.
3 Combine sugar and
extra water in a small
pan. Stir constantly over
low heat until mixture
boils and sugar has
dissolved. Reduce heat,
simmer, uncovered,
without stirring,
3 minutes or until
golden. Remove from
heat, add cream and
nuts, stir until
combined. Spoon into
pastry cases; cool.

Note: Pastry cases can
be made up to 3 days
ahead. Filling can be
added a day ahead.
Store in airtight container.
◆ Unsuitable to freeze.

Date and Pecan Pinwheels

Preparation time:
30 minutes
Cooking time:
10 minutes
Makes about 30

1 cup chopped pitted
dates
2 tablespoons sugar
1/4 cup water
2 tablespoons chopped
pecan nuts
3 oz butter
1/2 cup brown sugar
1 egg yolk

1¹/2 cups all-purpose
flour
1/2 teaspoon ground
pumpkin pie spice
1/4 teaspoon baking soda
1 tablespoon milk

1 Preheat oven to
moderate 350°F. Brush
baking sheets with
melted butter or oil.
Combine dates, sugar
and water in a medium
pan, stir over medium
heat for 2 minutes or
until water is absorbed.
Remove dates from
heat, stir in nuts, cool.
2 Using electric beaters,
beat butter and brown
sugar in small mixing
bowl until light and
creamy. Add egg yolk,
beat until combined.
3 Add sifted flour, spice,
baking soda and milk.
Press together to form a
soft dough. Turn onto
lightly floured surface,
knead 2 minutes until
smooth. Leave, covered
with plastic wrap, in
refrigerator 30 minutes.
4 Roll out onto lightly
floured surface to a
rectangle 8 x 11 inches.
Spread evenly with date
mixture. Roll up from
the long side. Wrap in
plastic wrap, freeze
30 minutes.
5 Using a sharp knife
cut log into 1/2 inch-
thick rounds. Place on
prepared baking sheets,

Clockwise from left: Caramel Nut Tarts, Date and
Pecan Pinwheels, Christmas Bells (p. 50)

allowing room for spreading. Bake for 10 minutes or until lightly browned. Cool on baking sheets.

Note: Store in airtight container for one week.
◆ Pinwheels can be frozen for up to 2 months.
◆ You can vary the fruit and nut mixture. Raisins, mixed candied citrus peel, prunes or golden raisins can replace the dates, and walnuts, almonds or hazelnuts can be substituted for pecans.

Christmas Bells

Preparation time:
  30 minutes + 10 minutes refrigeration
Cooking time:
  10 minutes
Makes about 50

4 oz butter
³/4 cup sugar
1 egg
1³/4 cups all-purpose flour
1 teaspoon ground cinnamon

¹/4 cup cocoa powder
sugar for sprinkling

To attach bells to tree
33 ft x ¹/8 inch ribbon

1 Preheat oven to moderately hot 415°F. Brush baking sheets with melted butter or oil. Using electric beaters, beat butter and sugar in small mixing bowl until light and creamy. Add egg, beat until combined.
2 Divide mixture between 2 small bowls. Add 1 cup sifted flour

1. *Christmas Bells. Beat butter and sugar, add egg, beat until combined.*

2. *Add remaining sifted four and cocoa to half egg, butter and sugar mixture.*

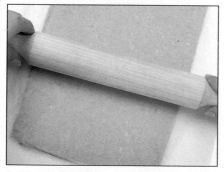

3. *Use a rolling pin to press the two mixtures together.*

4. *Cut mixture into bell shapes, cut a hole in top of each bell.*

and cinnamon to one half, mix to a soft dough. Add remaining sifted flour and cocoa to remaining half, mix to a soft dough. Store, covered with plastic wrap, in refrigerator 10 minutes.

3 Roll each mixture between 2 sheets of waxed paper to form rectangles, each measuring 8 x 12 inches. Remove top sheets of paper from each, invert one onto the other. Use rolling pin to press the 2 mixtures together, remove paper.

4 Cut into bell shapes using a cookie cutter. Place onto prepared baking sheets, allowing room for spreading, half with chocolate side facing up, remaining half with cinnamon side facing up.

5 Pile scraps on top of one another, roll out, cut into shapes, place onto prepared baking sheets. Use a straw or small

sharp pointed knife to make a hole in the top of each bell. Sprinkle bells with sugar. Bake for 10 minutes or until just golden, loosen bells, cool on baking sheets.

6 Cut ribbon into 8 inch lengths, thread through hole in top of bells, tie ends together in a knot.

Note: Bells can be made 3 days ahead, store in an airtight container.
◆ Bells made from the second rolling have a mottled appearance.
◆ Any shaped cutters can be used, e.g. stars, Santas, triangles and animals.
◆ Can be frozen for up to 2 months.

> HINT
> Use Christmas Bells to decorate your Christmas tree and let the kids have fun eating them during the festive season.

Florentine Slice

Preparation time:
15 minutes
Cooking time:
25 minutes
Makes 28

2 cups corn flakes, lightly crushed
1/2 cup golden raisins
1/2 cup sliced almonds
1/2 cup chopped glacé cherries
1/4 cup mixed candied citrus peel
2/3 cup condensed milk
4 oz dark chocolate, melted

1 Preheat oven to moderate 350°F. Brush an 11 1/2 x 7 1/2 x 1 1/4 inch jelly roll pan with melted butter or oil. Line base and sides with waxed paper, grease paper.

2 Combine corn flakes, golden raisins, almonds, cherries and peel. Add milk, combine.

5. Sprinkle bells with sugar. Bake for 10 minutes.

6. Thread ribbon through each hole, tie ends in knot.

3 Press mixture evenly into prepared tin. Bake for 25 minutes or until lightly browned, cool 5 minutes, turn out.
4 Cut into 4 x 4 cm squares. Hold each square by one corner, dip square halfway into chocolate. Allow excess to run off, place onto wire rack to set.

Note: Slice can be stored in an airtight container in refrigerator for up to 1 week.
◆ Unsuitable to freeze.

Mini Festive Fruit Cakes

Preparation time:
   15 minutes
Cooking time: 1 hour
Makes six 2-cup tins

6 cups mixed fruit
1 cup glacé cherries, halved
250 g butter
1 cup brown sugar
1 cup water
5 eggs, lightly beaten
1 tablespoon grated orange rind
1 3/4 cups plain flour
1/3 cup self-raising flour
1 teaspoon bicarbonate of soda

1 Preheat the oven to slow 150C. Brush 6 x (2-cup) or 12 x (1-cup) fluted tins all over with melted butter or oil if you prefer.
2 Combine mixed fruit, cherries, butter, sugar and water in a large saucepan. Stir over high heat until mixture boils, reduce heat to a simmer, cook, covered, for 10 minutes, stirring occasionally, cool.
3 Add eggs and rind. Stir until combined. Add sifted plain and self-raising flours and soda. Using a metal spoon, stir until just combined.
4 Spoon the mixture into the prepared tins, smooth surface. Bake for 1 hour or until the cakes feel firm and are a lovely golden brown. Allow the cakes to cool in the tins.

Note: Half the water can be replaced with rum, brandy or sherry.
◆ This mixture is enough to fill 4 nut roll tins.
◆ These cakes can be wrapped and stored in an airtight container for up to 1 month.

HINT
These cakes make lovely gifts when they're wrapped in cellophane and tied up with a ribbon.

Grand Marnier Semolina Fruit Cake

Preparation time:
   20 minutes plus overnight soaking
Cooking time: 4 hours
Makes one 23 cm round or one 20 cm square cake

1 1/2 cups raisins, finely chopped
1 1/2 cups sultanas, finely chopped
1 cup mixed peel, finely chopped
1 cup finely chopped glacé apricots
1/2 cup currants
1/2 cup glacé ginger, finely chopped
1/2 cup Grand Marnier
1 1/2 cups semolina
1 teaspoon ground cinnamon
1 teaspoon ground cardamom
185 g butter
4 eggs
1 cup brown sugar
1/2 cup marmalade
1/4 cup honey
3 teaspoons grated orange rind
1/3 cup orange juice
1 cup slivered almonds

1 Preheat oven to slow 150°C. Brush a deep,

Clockwise from top left: Mini Festive Fruit Cakes, Grand Marnier Semolina Fruit Cake, Florentine Slice (p. 51)

9 inch round or a deep, 8 inch square cake pan with melted butter or oil. Line base and sides with a double thickness of waxed paper.

2 Combine raisins, golden raisins, peel, apricots, currants, ginger and Grand Marnier in a bowl, cover with plastic wrap, stand overnight.

3 Stir semolina in a saucepan over medium heat for 5 minutes or until lightly browned. Add cinnamon, cardamom and butter, stir over heat until butter has melted, cool, cover with plastic wrap, stand overnight.

4 Using electric beaters, beat eggs and sugar in small mixing bowl until pale and foamy. Add marmalade, honey, orange rind and juice, beat until combined.

5 Transfer mixture to large mixing bowl, add fruits, semolina mixture and almonds. Using a metal spoon, stir until just combined.

6 Spoon mixture into prepared pan, smooth surface. Bake for 1 hour. Cover cake with a sheet of aluminum foil, reduce heat to very slow 250°F. Bake further 3 hours or until cake feels firm and is golden brown. Cool in pan completely. Turn out, wrap cake so it is airtight, and store.

Note: Dried fruits can be chopped in a food processor. Process each fruit individually. Be careful not to over-process or fruit will become mushy.

Traditional Fruit Cake

Preparation time:
  20 minutes plus 4 hours soaking
Cooking time:
  3 hours
Makes one 9 inch round or one 8 inch square cake

6 *cups dried mixed fruit*
1 1/2 *cups chopped dried dates*
1 *cup chopped dried apricots*
1 *cup chopped glacé pineapple*
3/4 *cup brandy*
8 *oz butter*
1 *cup brown sugar*
5 *eggs*
1 1/2 *cups all-purpose flour*
1/3 *cup self-rising flour*
1 *teaspoon ground cinnamon*
blanched almonds for decoration
glacé cherries, for decoration

1 Preheat oven to slow 300°F. Brush a deep 9 inch round or a deep

8 inch square cake pan with melted butter or oil. Line base and sides with a double thickness of waxed paper.

2 Combine mixed fruit, dates, apricots, pineapple and brandy, cover with plastic wrap, stand at least 4 hours.

3 Using electric beaters, beat butter and sugar in mixing bowl until light and creamy. Add eggs gradually, beating after each addition.

4 Transfer mixture to large mixing bowl, add fruits, stir until combined. Using a metal spoon, fold in sifted flour, self-rising flour and cinnamon. Stir until just combined.

5 Spoon mixture into prepared pan, smooth surface. Decorate with almonds and cherries. Bake for 3 hours or until cake feels firm and is golden brown. Cool slightly, turn out and cool completely. Wrap airtight and store.

Note: This cake can be wrapped and stored in an airtight container for up to 3 months.

> HINT
> For extra flavor, drizzle 1/4 cup brandy over cake after removing it from oven.

Traditional Fruit Cake

Christmas Crafts

Christmas Tree Decorations

These hand-made felt Christmas decorations are great fun to make (the children can help), and are original and long-lasting. They could end up becoming Christmas heirlooms.

All decorations
colored felt
embroidery thread in
  black and colors to
  match the felt
sequins and lace flowers
polyester fiber filling
gold thread or ribbon
  for hanging

1 Follow instructions on page 60 to enlarge patterns. Make patterns for all decorative felt shapes and allow a $1^1/4$ inch seam on edges that are to be inserted on main shapes—mane and tail of the horse, comb of the hen and base of the tree.
2 Cut pieces from felt as described for each. Tack inserted pieces to wrong side of one main piece. Join main pieces using hand buttonhole-stitch in embroidery thread or with narrow machine zig-zag. Fill lightly before closing completely.
3 Stitch or glue decorations in place. Work embroidery, then thread tie with a large needle.

Chicken
Cut two of body and one each of comb and decorative pieces. Cut decorative pieces for other side if you like.

Cat
Cut two of body and one each of stripe and flower. Tie gold thread in a bow around neck.

Tree
Cut two each of tree and base, and one heart. Stitch a base to each tree piece, then make as main piece.

House
Cut two each of house, window and sill, and one each of door and roof. Add roof and decorations after joining and filling main pieces.

1 sq = ¹/₂ inch

Horse

Cut two each of body and heart, one saddle on fold, one mane and a 2 x ^{5}/8 inch tail. Cut end of tail in strips. Embroider eye on each side of head. Decorate saddle with a flower and heart.

Hearts and Flowers Tree

Gold pine cones and basket

Use gold spray paint and follow manufacturer's instructions to spray pine cones. Wear rubber gloves, as it is hard to avoid touching the cones while painting. When dry, attach cones to the tree with wire. Spray a large cane basket gold as a container for the bucket holding your tree.

Gold garlands

These are gold curling ribbons loosely draped over the tree.

Angel

sheet of gold cardboard
pack of gold doilies
  with lacy edge pattern
2^1/2 inch white
  polystyrene ball, or
  florist's foam ball, for
  head
11 inch-long, 1^1/3 inch-
  wide cardboard cylinder
  (from plastic wrap)
gold curling ribbon
stapler
double-sided adhesive
  tape

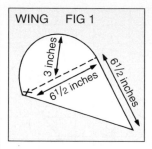

compass
ruler

1 Following Fig. 1, make pattern for the wing, using compass and ruler.
2 On gold cardboard, draw a 12 inch-radius semi-circle and a concentric 1^1/4 inch-radius semi-circle; cut out this piece for body. Cut out two wings, a 20 x 2 inch strip for arms and a 2^1/2 x 1^1/4 inch piece to join the wings.
3 Overlap straight edges of body and join with double-sided adhesive tape. Insert cardboard cylinder through small neck opening, clipping neck edge for exact fit. Staple the edges together.
4 Stick center of arm strip to back seam, about 2^3/4 inches from neck. Curve the arms to front and attach the ends to the angel's body on each side.
5 Cut one doily in half and arrange around

neck, stapling at back. Cut the decorative edge from a doily and drape over arms, sticking at back. Retain one doily for halo and cut the lacy edge from the rest to staple to edges of wings and lower edge of body. Attach wings to joining piece at X, then stick them to the back seam just above the arms.
6 Draw features on ball with felt-tipped pens or colored pencils. Attach eight 16 inch lengths of curling ribbon to top of head with staple. Stick head to neck then stick the doily behind the head to form a halo.
7 To fix to tree, either push cylinder over tip of tree or, for extra support, tape cylinder to a length of dowel which you can attach to the tree with wire.

Paper poinsettias

For about 28 flowers:
1 pack crepe paper
1 sheet red cellophane
1 roll 7-strand picture
  wire or fine
  gold-colored wire
about 200 small
  sequins
fine wire-cutting pliers
stapler

1 Following instructions overleaf for

Hearts and Flowers Tree

58

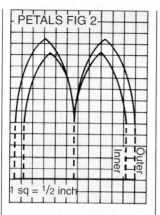

PETALS FIG 2

Inner | Outer

1 sq = ½ inch

HEART BASKET

FIG 4

RED

GOLD

FIG 3

1½ inches

3¼ inches

WEAVE THROUGH EACH LOOP

¾ inch ¾ inch ¾ inch ¾ inch

Fold

enlarging patterns, enlarge patterns for the petals, Fig. 2.

2 Fold crepe paper to the same width as large petal pattern and cut continuous strips of large petals. Do the same with cellophane and small paper pattern. Cut the petals into groups of six.

3 To make stamens, cut wire into 4 inch lengths, unwind one end of each piece of wire and attach a sequin to each strand, twisting twice with pliers to hold sequin. Or make up separate stamens from the fine wire and twist them together in groups of seven or more. Unravel some 4 inch lengths of wire to tie the flower petals in place.

4 To assemble flower, moisten straight edge of cellophane petals with a damp tissue to make them more pliable,

bunch around stamen wire and staple to hold. Gather crepe petals at base, arrange around cellophane, tie with wire. Holding sides of crepe petals, stretch each petal and push out its center. Use the end of stamen wire to fasten the flowers to the tree.

Heart Baskets
For about 14 hearts:
1 sheet each red and gold firm, shiny gift-wrapping paper

cardboard
adhesive tape or stapler
scissors
metal straightedge
craft knife
compass
ruler

1 Using ruler and compass, draw pattern, Fig. 3 on cardboard and cut out, using craft knife and straightedge for straight lines.
2 With pattern on fold on paper, cut, for each heart, one red and one

HOW TO ENLARGE PATTERNS

On a sheet of paper, draw crisscross lines, vertically and horizontally, using a ruler and spacing lines as indicated. Copy one square at a time, using a ruler for straight lines. For curved lines, mark where lines intersect grid, and join.

old piece and a $^3/4$ x
$5^1/2$ inch strip for
handle. While pieces are
folded, make the 3 cuts
with craft knife and
straightedge. You can
use scissors, but the
craft knife is much
quicker and neater.
3 Following Fig. 4,
weave strips together
to form basket. Staple
or stick end of handle
securely to each side of
the basket on the inside.
4 Tie heart baskets to
tree with yarn or wire.

Christmas Topiary Tree

This little tree is made
from ribbon bows.
You could also use
fabric cut with pinking
shears and tied into
bows, or tulle bunches.

ribbon bows in red,
white and green
tree branch or
doweling
plastic plant pot
polystyrene ball
(available from florist
or craft shops)
firm florists's wire
(available from florist
or craft shops)
plaster of Paris
(available from
hardware stores)

1 Select a small tree
branch for the trunk
(or use a length of
doweling), sharpen
one end and push the
oasis ball firmly onto

it. Cover the holes in
the bottom of the pot
with plastic. Following
directions on the bag,
mix the plaster. Spoon
plaster into pot and
stand the tree trunk
in the plaster. Hold
steady until set.
2 Wind florist's wire
firmly around center of
each bow, and push end
into the oasis ball. It is

important to get a good
shape for the tree, so
start by placing a top,
bottom and two side
bows to get the width
of the tree. Turn tree
around as you shape it,
pushing bows in a little
further or pulling them
out a little to create the
perfect shape.
3 Wire another large
bow, push into base of

61

ball and allow ribbon to fall down the trunk.
4 Place tree in a painted basket and arrange colored fabric around the base to hide the cement in the pot.

Shave Kit

Size: about 6 x 7 x 1¹/4 inches

13¹/2 x 21¹/4 inch piece of blue stripe fabric
7 x 22¹/2 inch piece of blue print fabric
18¹/2 x 46 inch-wide waterproof lining fabric (or nylon shower curtain fabric)
iron-on interfacing
12 inch zipper
6 x 12 inch stiff cardboard
⁵/8 inch seams allowed

1 From print fabric, cut two 7 inch square end pieces and one 3 x 7 inch strip. From lining, cut one 13¹/2 x 21¹/4 inch body, two 7 inch square ends, one 13¹/2 inch square. From interfacing, cut one 13¹/2 x 21¹/4 inch body, two 7 inch square ends.
2 Fuse interfacing to stripe body and end pieces. Baste lining to print end pieces. Baste a 2 inch box pleat at center top of each end piece.
3 Fold 3 x 7 inch strip of print fabric lengthways right sides together. Seam, turn and cut in

half. Fold in half for tabs. Baste one, centered, over each pleat, matching raw edges.
4 With right sides together, center and stitch zipper (¹/4 inch seam) to 13¹/2 inch edges of body. Stitch print end pieces to body, right sides together, with zipper centered over tabs and clipping and pivoting at the corners.
5 With right sides together and edges even, pin lining to wrong side of zipper tapes. Stitch over previous stitching up to ⁵/8 inch from end pieces. Turn, machine-stitch lining close to each of end pieces, clipping at corners.
6 Fold 13¹/2 inch square in half and stitch any two edges, turn right side out and turn in raw edges. Insert cardboard and stitch opening. Put into bag as a base.

Tote Bag

Size: 15 x 12 inch self-lined

5 ft teal blue sailcloth o furnishing fabric
20 inch red sprig cottor red and yellow remnants
10 inch heavyweight interfacing
¹/2 inch seams allowed

1 Draw a heart on tracing paper, 4¹/4 inche down its center length. Transfer to cardboard; cut out. Trace heart onto red remnant and cut ¹/4 inch outside line. Tack heart shape, right side up, over cardboard Press, remove tacking and cardboard.
2 Cut 9 inch square yellow pocket, hem ³/4 inch top edge. Center heart on pocket, slipstitch.

3 From teal blue fabric, cut 16 x 59 inch bag bodies, two 6 x 24³/4 inch sides. With right sides together, seam 16 inch ends together for center bottom. Make marks 2³/4 inches and 26³/4 inches from both sides of seam, clip ¹/2 inch at marks.
4 Match corners of one side piece to marks on body side, right sides together. Pin and sew all around. Repeat at

other side, leaving 8 inches open. Turn bag through opening, slipstitch closed. Push half of bag inside other half to form self-lining (sides are 12 inches high). Press fold at top edge. Baste pocket to center top on one side.
5 Cut 4 inch-wide sprig strips, seam to make 8.5 ft ring for handle. Cut and seam interfacing the same way. Fold sprig strip

around interfacing, turning raw edge under, slipstitch. Make another 9 inch sprig strip the same way, slipstitch to pocket bottom (see photograph), overlapping ⁵/8 inch. Mark halves of handle ring. Position on bag so marks are on center bottom seam, 7¹/2 inches apart (handles overlap pocket sides ⁵/8 inch). Slipstitch in place.

63

Index